BIG
ART
KNITS

BY EMILY GUISE

Printed in the United States of America

First Printing, 2015

ISBN 978-1-62767-099-9

Versa Press, Inc
800-447-7829

www.versapress.com

CONTENTS

INTRODUCTION

When I began designing this collection, I was inspired by texture, the geometric art of mid-20th-century artists, and a home filled with cozy, handmade things, and the beauty of bulky and super bulky yarns. These yarns highlight the texture of even the most basic knit and purl stitches, and the easy patterns knit up quickly and beautifully.

I named each pattern after a different artist, like Sonia Delaunay, who used lines and color to convey energy, or Donald Judd, who pared a shape down to its most elemental. I translated their visions into modern, versatile and functional pillows, throws, an ottoman cover, a rug, and even a wall hanging. These pieces will add an artistic touch to any home, and I hope you enjoy making them as much as I did designing them!

—Emily

BOCCIONI PILLOW

FINISHED MEASUREMENTS

14" Square

YARN

Knit Picks Big Cozy (55% Superfine
Alpaca, 45% Peruvian Highland Wool; 44
yards/100g): Finnley Heather 26488, 5 balls.
Knit Picks Imagination (50% Merino Wool,
25% Superfine Alpaca, 25% Nylon; 438
yards/100g): Bare 26589, 1 hank (optional).

NEEDLES

US 17 (12mm) 24" circular needles, or size to
obtain gauge

NOTIONS

Yarn Needle
Stitch Markers
14" Square Pillow Form

GAUGE

7 sts and 11 rows = 4" over Loop Stitch
Pattern in the round, blocked.

Boccioni Pillow

Notes:

This fluffy, loopy pillow is a perfect accent piece for a cozy couch or bed. Be careful when making the loops to keep them roughly the same size for a uniform look. The pillow is knit inside out and in the round, so while knitting the loops are on the wrong side. After the bind-off, the cover is flipped inside out, so the loops are on the front and the cozy reverse stockinette is on the back. If you'd like, hold Imagination with the Big Cozy to add interesting texture and contrast to the pillow. You may knit the entire pillow this way or choose to do just a few rounds- it's up to you!

Loop Stitch Pattern (in the round over any number of sts)
Rounds 1-4: Knit.
Round 5: *Holding 3rd finger of left hand over yarn behind work, K1 (so yarn forms loop about 3" long around finger) but do not sl this st from needle; transfer the st just worked back onto left-hand needle and K2tog TBL (the st just knitted, and the original st); then remove finger from loop to make another loop in the next st as before; rep from * in every st.
Round 6: K TBL every st.

DIRECTIONS

CO 48 sts. Join into round, being careful not to twist sts. PM.

Begin Loop Stitch for 24 sts, PM, K the next 24 sts.

Continue as established, repeating Loop Stitch over first 24 sts and K the remaining 24. When desired, begin knitting with Imagination held with Big Cozy.

Once the piece measures 14", ending on a K round, BO all sts.

Finishing

Weave in ends and block to finished measurements. Flip piece inside out so the loops are on the outside. Sew one end shut using mattress st. Insert the pillow form. Using mattress st or whipstitch, close the opening over the pillow.

HESSE BLANKET

FINISHED MEASUREMENTS

31 x 47" throw, 55 x 60" blanket

YARN

Knit Picks Biggo (50% Superwash Merino
Wool, 50% Nylon); Brass Heather 26571, (9),
18 hanks

NEEDLES

US 15 (10mm) 32" circular needles, or size to
obtain gauge

NOTIONS

Yarn Needle
Stitch Markers

GAUGE

7.5 sts and 11.25 rows = 4" in Hesse Stitch
Pattern with yarn held double, blocked.

Hesse Blanket

Notes:

A luxuriously soft and cozy blanket to snuggle up under, the Hesse Blanket features an alternating drop stitch pattern that's easy to memorize but never boring. Biggo is held doubled so the knitting goes twice as fast. Directions for the throw are in parentheses. This blanket is named for Eva Hesse, a groundbreaking mid-20th century sculptor known for her pioneering work with materials such as fiberglass, latex, and plastic, reflecting both fluid spontaneity and repetition.

Hesse Stitch Pattern (worked flat over multiples of 9 sts plus 4)

Rows 1, 3, 5 (WS): P1, * K2, P2, K2, P3; rep from * to last 3 sts, K2, P1.

Rows 2 and 4 (RS): K1, *P2, K3, P2, K2; rep from * to last 3 sts, P2, K1.

Row 6: K1, *P2, K1, drop next st off needle and unravel to YO 6 rows below, K1, P2, K1, YO, K1; rep from * to last 3 sts, P2, K1.

Rows 7, 9 and 11: P1, *K2, P3, K2, P2; rep from * to last 3 sts, K2, P1.

Rows 8 and 10: K1, *P2, K2, P2, K3; rep from * to last 3 sts, P2, K1.

Row 12: K1, *P2, K1, YO, K1, P2, K1, drop next st off needle and unravel to YO 6 rows below, K1; rep from * to last 3 sts, P2, K1.

Rep Rows 1-12 for pattern.

DIRECTIONS

With yarn held double, CO 52 (92) sts.

Set Up Row (RS): K1, *P2, K1, YO, K1, P2, K2; rep from * to last 3 sts, P2, K1. 58 (103) sts.

Begin Row 1 of Hesse Stitch Pattern.

Repeat Hesse Stitch Pattern 11 (14) times, for a total of 132 (168) rows.

BO all sts K-wise.

Finishing

Weave in ends, wash and block to finished measurements.

CARR CUSHION

FINISHED MEASUREMENTS

16" square

YARN

Knit Picks Big Cozy (55% Superfine
Alpaca, 45% Peruvian Highland Wool; 44
yards/100g): Bare 26483, 6 balls.

NEEDLES

US 36 (20mm) 24" circular needles, or size
to obtain gauge

NOTIONS

Yarn Needle
Small length of yarn in contrasting color (for
marker)
16" Square Pillow Form

GAUGE

4.5 sts and 7 rounds = 4" over St st in the
round with yarn held doubled, blocked.

Carr Cushion

Notes:

Supersized bobbles float diagonally over a sea of reverse stockinette for maximum visual punch. The Big Cozy is held double-stranded to get that supersized look. The pattern is knit in the round inside out to minimize purling, then turned right side out and the top and bottom are sewn shut. This cozy cushion is named after Emily Carr, one of the first modernist Canadian artists.

Cable Cast On

Make a backwards loop, with the working yarn on top. Place loop on right hand needle and tighten gently.

Make Bobble (MB)

Place right hand needle into next st as if to K, Cable Cast On 3 sts, then knit original st. Turn work WYIB. K these 4 sts. Turn WYIF. BO 3 sts, 1 st remains. Sl this st to right hand needle WYIB.

You will hold the yarn doubled while knitting the entire piece, including the bobble.

DIRECTIONS

With yarn held double, CO 36 sts. Join into a round, being careful not to twist, and PM (a different colored piece of yarn tied into a circle is a great marker for these giant needles).

Rnds 1-5: Knit.
Rnd 6: K2, MB, K to end of rnd.
Rnds 7-11: Knit.
Rnd 12: K7, MB, K to end of rnd.
Rnds 13-17: Knit.
Rnd 18: K11, MB, K to end of rnd.
Rnds 19-22: Knit.
Rnd 23: K14, MB, K to end of rnd.
Rnds 24-28: Knit.

BO all sts.

Finishing

Turn work inside out so bobbles and reverse St st are on outside. Weave in ends and block to finished measurements.

Using mattress stitch, sew the top opening shut. Insert the pillow form. Use mattress stitch or whipstitch to sew the bottom opening shut.

JUDD CUBE

FINISHED MEASUREMENTS
18" high, wide, and long

YARN
Knit Picks Brava (100% Premium Acrylic);
Solstice Heather 25732, 12 skeins for cover,
15 skeins for complete cube

NEEDLES
US 15 (10mm) 32" circular needles, or size to
obtain gauge

NOTIONS
Yarn Needle

GAUGE
7.5 sts and 9 rows = 4" in Garter st with yarn
held tripled, blocked

Judd Cube

Notes:

Dress up an ottoman with this easy, subtly textured cover. It's knit separately in five pieces and sewn together for a cover to fit over an ottoman. You can also make an extra panel and stuff it for a complete cube, perfect for extra seating. The pattern is named after Donald Judd, an American minimalist artist who often worked with cubes and other rectilinear forms.

DIRECTIONS

With yarn held tripled, CO 34 sts.

Rows 1-5: K all sts.
Row 6: Purl.
Repeat Rows 1-6 until piece measures 18" high, ending with a P row.

BO all sts.

Repeat for each square, until you have five squares for the ottoman cover, six if you want a complete cube.

Finishing

Weave in ends, wash and block to finished measurements. Using mattress stitch, sew the vertical edges of four squares together (see diagram) with the purled rows horizontal. Then sew the fifth square on top of the other four.

For the complete cube, after seaming the five squares stuff an old comforter or two in and sew the sixth square on top. For the final edge,, whipstitching it shut may be easier than mattress stitch.

Assembling the Cube

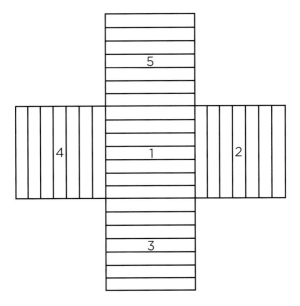

DELAUNAY PILLOW

FINISHED MEASUREMENTS

16" square

YARN

Knit Picks Wool of the Andes Superwash
Bulky (100% Superwash Wool, 137
yds/100g): C1 White 26522, C2 Dove
Heather 26505; 1 hank each. C3 Hollyberry
26510, 3 hanks.

NEEDLES

US 15 (10mm) needles, or size to obtain
gauge

NOTIONS

Yarn Needle
16" Square Pillow Form

GAUGE

8.5 sts and 14 rows = 4" over Garter St with
yarn held doubled, blocked.

Delaunay Pillow

Notes:

The sharp angles of this pillow was influenced by the art of Sonia Delaunay, who often worked in bright colors and geometric shapes as a painter and textile designer. The front triangles and the back square are all knitted separately and sewn together with mattress stitch. Colorful and versatile Wool of the Andes Superwash Bulky is held double so these pieces knit up quickly.

DIRECTIONS

Large Triangle

Using C3 and with yarn held double, CO 3 sts.

Row 1: K1, KFB, K1. 4 sts.
Row 2: K1, KFB, K to end of row.

Repeat Row 2 until the long side of triangle measures 22.5". BO all sts.

Small Triangle (make 2)

Using C2 and with yarn held double, CO 3 sts.

Row 1: K1, KFB, K1. 4 sts.
Row 2: K1, KFB, K to end of row.

Repeat Row 2 until the long side of triangle measures 16".

Using C1, make another triangle as above.

Square

Using C3 and with yarn held double, CO 34 sts. Knit every row until piece measures 16" long. BO all sts.

Finishing

Weave in ends and block pieces to measurements in schematic. Using mattress or whip stitch, sew triangles together as in Pillow Assembly diagram, then sew three sides of square to the triangles. Insert pillow form and whip stitch the opening shut.

Small Triangle

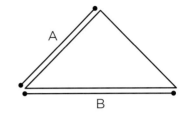

Large Triangle

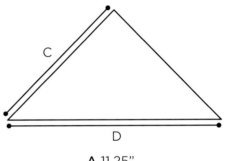

A 11.25"
B 16"
C 16"
D 22.5"

Pillow Assembly

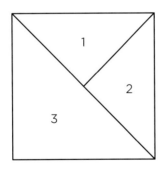

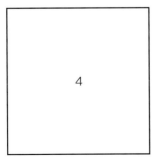

Sew triangle 1 to 2, then sew both to 3. Sew square 4 to three sides of front. Insert pillow form. Sew opening shut.

SERRA RUG

FINISHED MEASUREMENTS
36" wide x 21" high

YARN
Knit Picks Brava Bulky (100% Premium Acrylic; 136 yards/100g): Silver 26390, 7 balls.

NEEDLES
US 15 (10mm) 24" circular needles, or size to obtain gauge

NOTIONS
Yarn Needle
Stitch Markers
Rug Pad (optional)

GAUGE
7.5 sts and 12 rows = 4" in Ridge Lattice pattern with yarn held tripled, blocked.

Serra Rug

Notes:
This cushy rug has reverse stockinette ridges with a great texture that contrasts beautifully with the lines of slip stitches. Knitted flat on Brava held tripled, this rug is a fast and satisfying project. It's named after minimalist artist Richard Serra, a sculptor who creates enormous life-size interactive sculptures made of flat sheet metal.

Slip all sts P-wise.

Ridge Lattice Pattern (worked flat over multiples of 4 sts plus 3)
Row 1 (WS): Purl.
Row 2 (RS): K1, *Sl1 WYIB, K3; rep from * to last two sts, Sl1, K1.
Row 3: Purl.
Row 4: K1, *Sl1 WYIB, P3; rep from * to last two sts, Sl1, K1.
Rows 5-8: Rep Rows 3-4, twice.
Row 9: Purl.
Row 10: Rep Row 2.

Rep Rows 1-10 for pattern.

Backwards Loop Cast On
Start with a slipknot on your needle. Hold your needle in your right hand and use your fingers to keep the yarn tail out of the way. Grasp the working yarn in your left hand.

Pass the working yarn around your left thumb from back to front. Slip the needle tip under the loop around your thumb. Pull your thumb out of the loop and tug on the working yarn to tighten up the st.

See the tutorial at: http://tutorials.knitpicks.com/wptutorials/loop-cast-on/

DIRECTIONS
Holding three strands of yarn together, loosely CO 67 sts using a Backwards Loop CO.

Begin working Ridge Lattice pattern, and continue for 80 rows, repeating the Ridge Lattice pattern 8 times. BO all sts P-wise, loosely.

Finishing
Weave in ends, wash and block to finished measurements.

BRAQUE WALL HANGING

FINISHED MEASUREMENTS
12.5" wide x 17" high

YARN
Knit Picks Chroma Worsted (70% Wool, 30% Nylon; 198 yards/100g): Wildflower 26555, 1 ball.
Wool of the Andes Roving (100% Peruvian Wool Top Roving, 100g): Bare 25201, 1 package.

NEEDLES
US 11 (8mm) 24" circular needles (circulars are necessary for the project), or size to obtain gauge

NOTIONS
Yarn Needle
Dowel, 14" Knitting Needle or Stick for Hanging (optional)

GAUGE
10 sts and 20 rows = 4" over Garter St, blocked (Gauge is approximate, and not critical)

Braque Wall Hanging

Notes:

Instead of weaving a wall hanging, why not knit one? This decorative hanging uses fluffy roving to contrast with geometric stitch patterns, one of which slips the roving over and under the stitches so it appears woven. These loops of roving may be left loose for bigger loops or smaller for a tighter, more even look-it's up to you. Knit at a loose gauge, the beautiful graduation of color in Chroma contrast wonderfully with the creamy whiteness of the roving. Circular needles are necessary, as you'll be sliding the work back and forth. Feel free to start the project at the beginning of your favorite color, rather than using whatever one is at the start of the ball.

Cross Stitch Pattern (worked flat over multiples of 8 sts)

Row 1 (WS): *Insert needle into next st and wrap yarn 4 times around the needle point, then K the st, taking all of the wraps with the needle. Repeat from * on every st along row to last st.

Row 2 (RS): *Sl 8 sts WYIB, dropping the wraps so there are 8 long sts on right hand needle. Insert left hand needle into first 4 sts and pass them over the second 4 sts, keeping them on the needle. Return all sts to left hand needle and K the 8 sts as crossed. Rep from * on each group of 8 sts.

Preparing the Roving

Gently pull the roving apart into long strips about 1/4" wide. Roll each strip into a loose ball for easier management when knitting.

DIRECTIONS

CO 33 sts.

Row 1 (WS): Knit.

Row 2 (RS): With roving, K 1 st. Pull Chroma working yarn tightly around it to secure. Sl 1 sts P-wise WYIB, pull roving around back of Sl st and bring to front. Sl next Chroma st, pulling roving over front of Sl st and bringing roving to back. Continue "weaving" the roving in between the slipped Chroma sts until end of row. End with roving at front of work. Slide work back to other end of needles.

Row 3 (RS): Knit.

Row 4 (WS): Sl 1 st (Chroma) WYIB. Bring roving up and over the front of Sl st as before, pulling roving around to back. Sl next st and pull roving around back of it and to front as before. Continue to end of row. Slide work to other end of needles.

Row 5 (WS): Knit.

Row 6 (RS): Rep Row 2, cutting roving and leaving tail.

Rows 7-14: Work in Garter st (K all sts) for 8 rows.

Row 15 (RS): Rep Row 2, but when bringing the loops around the front sts, wrap them around two fingers to make them longer, then slip as usual. Cut roving, leaving tail.

Row 16 (RS): K to last two sts, K2tog. (32 sts)

Rows 17-18: Work Rows 1-2 of Cross Stitch Pattern.

Row 19: K to last st, KFB. (33 sts)

Rows 20-24: Rep Rows 2-6.

Row 25 (RS): K to last st, K2tog. (32 sts)

Rows 26-27: Work Rows 1-2 of Cross Stitch Pattern.

Row 28 (WS): K to last st, KFB. (33 sts)

Rep Rows 2-28 once more, then rep Rows 2-6 once. Knit 1 Row. BO all sts loosely.

Finishing

Carefully weave in ends of roving to back of work loosely, as well as any other loose ends.

Using a piece of Chroma at least 24" long, thread it through the yarn needle. On a flat surface, place the dowel, knitting needle or stick lengthwise above the BO. Starting at the first bound-off stitch, thread the yarn under the stitch and over the dowel, needle, or stick, and under the next BO stitch.

Continue until all BO stitches are secured, then cut yarn and tie at knot at the back. Tie knot at other end and cut excess yarn. Tie a long matching piece of yarn at either end for hanging.

For pattern support, contact customerservice@knitpicks.com

Abbreviations		M	marker		stitch	TBL	through back loop
BO	bind off	M1	make one stitch	RH	right hand	TFL	through front loop
cn	cable needle	M1L	make one left-leaning	rnd(s)	round(s)	tog	together
CC	contrast color		stitch	RS	right side	W&T	wrap & turn (see
CDD	Centered double dec	M1R	make one right-lean-	Sk	skip		specific instructions
CO	cast on		ing stitch	Sk2p	sl 1, k2tog, pass		in pattern)
cont	continue	MC	main color		slipped stitch over	WE	work even
dec	decrease(es)	P	purl		k2tog: 2 sts dec	WS	wrong side
DPN(s)	double pointed	P2tog	purl 2 sts together	SKP	sl, k, psso: 1 st dec	WYIB	with yarn in back
	needle(s)	PM	place marker	SL	slip	WYIF	with yarn in front
EOR	every other row	PFB	purl into the front and	SM	slip marker	YO	yarn over
inc	increase		back of stitch	SSK	sl, sl, k these 2 sts tog		
K	knit	PSSO	pass slipped stitch	SSP	sl, sl, p these 2 sts tog		
K2tog	knit two sts together		over		tbl		
KFB	knit into the front and	PU	pick up	SSSK	sl, sl, sl, k these 3 sts		
	back of stitch	P-wise	purlwise		tog		
K-wise	knitwise	rep	repeat	St st	stockinette stitch		
LH	left hand	Rev St st	reverse stockinette	sts	stitch(es)		

Knit Picks yarn is both luxe and affordable—a seeming contradiction trounced! But it's not just about the pretty colors; we also care deeply about fiber quality and fair labor practices, leaving you with a gorgeously reliable product you'll turn to time and time again.

THIS COLLECTION FEATURES

Big Cozy
Super Bulky Weight
55% Superfine Alpaca,
45% Peruvian Highland Wool

Biggo
Bulky Weight
50% Superwash Merino Wool,
50% Nylon

Chroma Worsted
Worsted Weight
70% Wool, 30% Nylon

Wool of the Andes Superwash Bulky
Bulky Weight
100% Superwash Wool

Brava Bulky
Bulky Weight
100% Premium Acrylic

Wool of the Andes Roving
100% Peruvian Wool Top Roving

View these beautiful yarns and
more at www.KnitPicks.com